Silly
Races

Written by Roderick Hunt

Illustrated by Alex Brychta

OXFORD

UNIVERSITY PRESS

Kipper ran.

Kipper got a banana.

8

Mum ran.

She got an apple.

Biff and Chip ran.

They got an orange.

Dad ran.

Floppy ran.

Oh no! Dad fell.

Dad got a duck!

Think about the story

Why are they
silly races?

Which race
do you think is
the funniest?

Which of
the races would you
like to be in?

What other
sorts of races
do people do?

Spot the difference

Find the 5 differences in the two paddling pools.